Aptis Advanced
MASTERCLASS

Speaking & Writing

Future House Languages
Online Language School | Publishing

aptisacademy**.com**™

Future House Languages
Online Language School | Publishing

Blasco de Garay 75, Madrid, 28003. Spain

Aptis Advanced
MASTERCLASS SPEAKING & WRITING

*HACK [HAK]

Noun

A hack is a clever solution that offers an easier way of doing or achieving something.

INTRODUCTION TO THIS BOOK

WHY APTIS?

The Aptis Advanced test is a British Council English exam which has gained popularity as a practical and accurate assessment of the English level of individuals in line with the CEFR (Common European Framework of Reference) scales. It is designed to differenciate beween high-level candidates (B2, C1 & C2).

The test is computer-based, which means that all sections of the test are taken with a computer and headphones, including the speaking section. Thanks to this, Aptis is an economical way to test your English, and your results are made quickly available. **The test includes the four main skills: reading, writing, speaking and listening - plus the compulsory core (grammar and vocabulary) section.**

Upon completion of the test you will be awarded a CEFR scale for the four main skills, a numerical score for each skill 0-50 and an overall level.

SAMPLE RESULTS CARD

SKILL NAME	SKILL SCORE	CEFR LEVEL
LISTENING	34/50	B2
READING	40/50	C1
SPEAKING	46/50	C1
WRITING	46/50	C1
FINAL SCALE SCORE	166	166
GRAMMAR & VOCABULARY	43/50	43/50

LEVEL
C1

 If you are between levels your grammar and vocabulary score will be taken into account. For this reason, the **grade boundaries are not exact,** so two people with the same score in a component could theoretically be awarded a different CEFR level due to having different grammar and vocabulary scores. A good score for C1 would be 40+/50.

HOW TO USE THIS BOOK

This book has been specially designed for self-study and includes everything you need to maximize your score and achieve your desired level in the speaking and writing components.

You will find all the materials that accompany this book on our e-learning platform. Create your account and access all the audios, tutorial videos, model answers for the writing and speaking component and more!

 Watch the tutorial videos on our e-learning platform for exam tips, secrets, expressions and model answers.

ACCOUNT INSTRUCTIONS

Create your account by following these easy steps.

1 Go to www.aptisacademy.com

2 Choose My Book on the homepage

3 Click on the book title you have purchased

4 Create your account with your email and username

5 Enter your UNIQUE CODE* in the coupon box at the checkout

6 Log in to your personal account and access all the interactive content

aeai6c55d1lhpsu

YOUR UNIQUE CODE

VOCABULARY GAMES

SCAN ME

Scan the QR codes **when you find them on pages in this book** to study the key vocabulary from that chapter.

You can access flashcards, memory games, quizzes and pronunciation all on your phone - a fantastic way to consolidate your learning and improve your English vocabulary.

*Your unique code is only given with the purchase of this book and is personal and non-transferable.

CORE COMPONENT

The core component is the same in all versions of the Aptis test (General, Teachers and Advanced).

The component is divided into <u>two</u> <u>sections</u> which test your knowledge of grammar and general English vocabulary.

This component lasts for 25 minutes.

Grammar

This section includes 25 questions with a choice of possible answers (A, B and C). You need to complete the sentence by choosing the correct option. Most of the questions test formal written English, but a few include spoken expressions in both informal and formal situations.

 You should study the explanations at the back of this book carefully, as any of the grammar structures covered in this book may appear in the real exam.

Vocabulary

This section consists of 25 questions and tests your knowledge of common vocabulary such as verbs, adjectives, nouns, collocations and phrasal verbs.

There are four common task-types: word matching, word definitions, word usage (how a word is used in context) and common collocations (words commonly used together by native speakers).

 The vocabulary section can seem quite overwhelming as you could be tested on any word from a bank of thousands of possible English words. For this reason, we have included QR codes with key vocabulary and collocations you should learn to help you maximize your score.

CORE COMPONENT: TEST 1

TEST 1: Grammar

Choose the correct answer (A, B or C)

1. I _____ to finish the report for tomorrow's meeting.

A hope

B wish

C remind

2. As _____ as they left the building, it started pouring with rain.

A sooner

B quicker

C soon

3. We regret _____ you that your request has been denied.

A for informing

B inform

C to inform

4. The theory explains _____ global warming is irreversible or not.

A why

B whether

C how

5. The manager insisted the last interviewee _____ the best candidate for the job.

A was

B has been

C will be

6. Customers are only _____ to smoke when eating out on the terrace.

A possible

B prohibited

C allowed

7. Each child _____ to bring the signed permission slip on the day of the field trip.

A has

B have

C must

8. A number of students _____ thanked the teacher after receiving their grades.

A have

B has

C will

9. Cristiano Ronaldo is _____ amazing football player.

A the

B a

C an

10. Simon has _____ fear of trying new foods.

A the

B none

C a

11. This story doesn't make sense, _____ must be lying.

A somebody

B nobody

C anybody

12. _____ a single word was spoken throughout the entire journey.

A None

B Not

C No

13. Even though she had very _____ money to spare, she gave the beggar some coins.

A few
B little
C only

14. _____wants to participate in the project must register before the end of the month.

A Whoever
B Who
C Whom

15. It's about time the government _____ in green energy.

A invest
B invested
C will invest

16. I _____ to call you, but I ran out of battery.

A was going
B am going
C am about

17. I can't believe Tom and Cindy _____ since last December.

A dating
B are dating
C have been dating

18. A: _____ I help you?
    B: No, thank you. I am just browsing.

A Would
B Will
C May

19. You _____ bring your computer, as we will provide you with one.

A shouldn't
B mustn't
C needn't

20. It's going to be a wonderful day, _____ it?

A isn't

B will

C won't

21. A: I'm quite tired.

   B: _____

A Too am I

B So am I

C I am so

22. How _____ did it take them to get to the airport?

A long

B far

C much

23. We _____ playing in the street.

A saw to them

B saw them to

C saw them

24. They usually sit _____ the table in the dining room to eat family dinners.

A at

B in

C on

25. This action movie is even _____ than the last one.

A most boring

B boringer

C more boring

TEST 1: Vocabulary

 Write the word from the list (A-J) which is most similar in meaning to the words on the left (1-5). Use each word only once. There are extra words which you will not need to use (A-J).

extend = spread

1. smile

2. laugh

3. surprise

4. harm

5. exchange

A. sob
B. return
C. shout
D. giggle
E. shock
F. please
G. hurt
H. grin
I. spread
J. swap

 Finish each definition (6-10) by using a word from the list (A-J). Use each word only once. There are extra words which you will not need to use (A-J).

To buy something is to...purchase

6. To respect is to...

7. To improve is to...

8. To breathe is to...

9. To attend is to...

10. To assess is to...

A. inhale
B. create
C. admire
D. purchase
E. examine
F. prepare
G. go
H. enhance
I. chew
J. evaluate

 Always read the instructions carefully as each task is different and read the list of words (A-J) before attempting to complete each task.

 Scan the QR code on this page to study the most challenging vocabulary from this section of the book.

SCAN ME

Write the word from the list (A-J) which matches the definition (11-15). There are extra words which you will not need to use (A-J).

Well-adapted for cutting... sharp

11. Very dirty…

12. Dependable…

13. Rapid, fast…

14. Rich, well-off…

15. Energy efficient; cheap to run…

A. economical
B. dusty
C. wealthy
D. surprised
E. **sharp**
F. filthy
G. spotless
H. reliable
I. thrilled
J. quick

 Finish each sentence (16-20) using a word from the list (A-J). Use each word only once. There are extra words which you will not need to use (A-J).

It hurts my back to sit on this <u>stool</u>. Can we move to a table with chairs?

16. The company will foot the _____ for all business trips.

17. We cannot jump to any _____ until we hear both sides of the story.

18. Would you like to _____ dinner with me after work?

19. She usually _____ into tears when she watches romantic movies.

20. They were going to sell their car, but they had a change of _____.

A. account
B. have
C. **stool**
D. take
E. conclusions
F. bursts
G. bill
H. heart
I. explodes
J. idea

 Write the word (A-J) that is most often used with a word on the list (21-25) to form a collocation. Use each word only once. There are extra words which you will not need to use (A-J).

private school

21. bright

22. heavy

23. sentimental

24. blatantly

25. breaking

A. light
B. metal
C. polite
D. obvious
E. road
F. **school**
G. news
H. shadow
I. value
J. opinion

TEST 2: Grammar

» **Choose the correct answer (A, B or C)**

1. Ana is staying with us at the moment. The children _____ her here.

A love have
B love having
C loved having

2. There is hardly _____ money left in our bank account!

A none
B little
C any

3. My mother just turned sixty-five which means she is _____ retire next year.

A due to
B about to
C on the verge of

4. The train to Saint Petersburg _____ at 9 a.m from platform six.

A leaves
B is leaving
C will leave

5. _____ the storm calms down, we should be able to take off on time.

A Despite
B Although
C Provided

6. It was the first time the employees _____ against the CEO's decision.

A protest
B will have protested
C had protested

7. Under no circumstances _____ open the door to strangers.

A should you
B you should
C should you to

8. The doctor will contact you _____ he has the test results.

A while
B as soon as
C as quickly as

9. You _____ walk the streets alone at night in this neighborhood - it's dangerous.

A mightn't
B don't have to
C shouldn't

10. Would you like _____ cheese?

A a little of
B a bit of
C a few of

11. Paris is _____ we first met.

A when
B that
C where

12. I was surprised to hear that Bruno Mars _____ in a musical on Broadway.

A is currently appearing
B currently appears
C will currently appear

13. After months of stressful work, Beth _____ quitting her job.

A considers

B will consider

C is considering

14. After she finished work, she _____ all afternoon sunbathing by the pool.

A spent

B had spent

C has spend

15. It's his third visit to the pool this week so he _____ enjoy swimming.

A ought to

B should

C must

16. I am sorry Mr. Smith has left the office, who _____ I say has called?

A should

B would

C have

17. He promised _____ that he would come to the party.

A to you

B you

C your

18. Who _____ the people sitting at that table?

A is

B was

C are

19. Sam switched easily between French and Spanish, _____ he spoke fluently.

A none of which

B both of which

C neither of which

20. We are looking forward to _____ your prompt reply.

A receiving
B receive
C have received

21. They will arrive this afternoon, _____ they?

A won't
B will
C aren't

22. You can't go swimming as the water is _____ freezing!

A very
B absolutely
C too

23. Speak softly _____ to wake up the kids.

A so as not
B not
C in order

24. _____ the pain in her knee, she was able to complete the race.

A Even if
B In spite of
C Although

25. I don't know _____, do you?

A where he is
B where is he
C he is where

TEST 2: Vocabulary

 Write the word from the list (A-J) which is most similar in meaning to the words on the left (1-5). Use each word only once. There are extra words which you will not need to use (A-J).

say = tell

1. award

2. income

3. assessment

4. price

5. sphere

A. fee
B. prize
C. priority
D. trial
E. tell
F. salary
G. scale
H. distance
I. evaluation
J. globe

 Finish each definition (6-10) by using a word from the list (A-J). Use each word only once. There are extra words which you will not need to use (A-J).

To be furious is...

6. To be drowsy is…

7. To be slim is…

8. To be complete is…

9. To be furry is…

10. To be gorgeous is…

A. thorough
B. obese
C. thin
D. angry
E. hairy
F. penniless
G. sleepy
H. beautiful
I. lax
J. cut

 Always read the instructions carefully as each task is different and read the list of words (A-J) before attempting to complete each task.

 Scan the QR code on this page to study the most challenging vocabulary from this section of the book.

Match each definition (11-15) to a word from the list (A-J). Use each word only once. There are extra words which you will not need to use (A-J).

> **To run at a leisurely, slow pace.**

11. To practise a work of art to perform in public.

12. To understand.

13. To apply yourself to the acquisition of knowledge.

14. To extend over a considerable area.

15. To move to action.

A. comprehend
B. spread
C. prompt
D. rehearse
E. jog
F. play
G. create
H. mirror
I. study
J. draw

 Finish each sentence (16-20) using a word from the list (A-J). Use each word only once. There are extra words which you will not need to use (A-J).

> **It hurts my back to sit on this <u>stool</u>. Can we move to a table with chairs?**

16. All that exercise has worked up my _____.

17. Due to constant arguing Glen and Jane have decided to file for _____.

18. The _____ are taking statements from the witnesses of the crime.

19. Tim has been humming a catchy _____ all morning.

20. I am not entirely sure how to solve the _____.

A. problem
B. song
C. statement
D. music
E. appetite
F. idea
G. solution
H. divorce
I. officers
J. stool

 Write the word (A-J) that is most often used with a word on the list (21-25) to form a collocation. Use each word only once. There are extra words which you will not need to use (A-J).

> **Close friend**

21. pay

22. ship

23. back

24. magnifying

25. light

A. nail
B. glass
C. rise
D. appeal
E. wreck
F. village
G. happiness
H. ache
I. bulb
J. friend

TEST 3: Grammar

» **Choose the correct answer (A, B or C)**

1. I refuse to attend the party _____ you come with me.

A however
B despite
C unless

2. I strongly recommend that you _____ in hospital for a few more days.

A stay
B stayed
C stays

3. Spring is my favourite season because our garden flowers _____ nice.

A are smelling
B smell
C scent

4. _____ something to eat?

A Is he wanting
B Do he wants
C Does he want

5. It _____ when we woke up this morning.

A was snowing
B has snowed
C snowed

6. She has lived in Portugal _____ 5 years.

A since

B until

C for

7. Have you _____ visited the Guggenheim Museum?

A never

B ever

C still

8. A: Why are you so tired?

B: _____ very hard.

A I have been working

B I had been working

C I worked

9. They haven't spoken to each other _____ 2005

A for

B in

C since

10. She should tell him the bad news, _____?

A should she

B shouldn't she

C doesn't she

11. We weren't tired as we _____ a nap before leaving.

A had taken

B take

C have taken

12. Kate _____ have short hair when she was younger.

A had

B would

C used to

13. Don't forget that your dentist appointment is _____ Tuesday afternoon.

A on

B in

C at

14. This time next week we _____ by the swimming pool.

A will sunbathe

B will be sunbathing

C have sunbathed

15. If you _____ rich, what would you spend your money on?

A are

B were

C will be

16. You look terrible. You _____ to bed early instead of going out all night.

A must have gone

B should have gone

C might have slept

17. The kids denied _____ the kitchen window with the ball.

A to break

B to breaking

C breaking

18. If they _____ you were so busy, they wouldn't have asked for your help.

A had known

B has known

C knew

19. If you practise more, you _____ pass your driving test.

A will

B would

C won't

20. Jim said he _____ 15 minutes late to this afternoon's meeting.

A would arrive
B arrived
C arrives

21. I wonder _____ to wait for the next bus.

A how long
B how long have we
C how long we have

22. Do you fancy _____ out tonight?

A to eat
B eating
C eat

23. Julie was tired, so she decided _____ at home and watch TV.

A to stay
B stay
C staying

24. A: Do you know what time it is?

B: As I'm not wearing a watch, _____.

A I'm afraid not
B I don't think so
C You shouldn't have

25. I've lived in the UK for 10 years, so _____ driving on the left.

A I used to
B I get used
C I am used to

TEST 3: Vocabulary

 Write the word from the list (A-J) which is most similar in meaning to the words on the left (1-5). Use each word only once. There are extra words which you will not need to use (A-J).

tip = hint

1. employees

2. boat

3. flame

4. client

5. book

A. fire
B. timber
C. tax
D. gear
E. ship
F. hint
G. customer
H. novel
I. vehicle
J. staff

 Finish each definition (6-10) by using a word from the list (A-J). Use each word only once. There are extra words which you will not need to use (A-J).

To buy something is to...purchase

6. To speak quietly is to...

7. To idolise is to...

8. To fight verbally is to...

9. To inundate is to...

10. To go back is to...

A. flood
B. pray
C. whisper
D. purchase
E. worship
F. sprint
G. chase
H. argue
I. return
J. calculate

 Always read the instructions carefully as each task is different and read the list of words (A-J) before attempting to complete each task.

 Scan the QR code on this page to study the most challenging vocabulary from this section of the book.

SCAN ME

Write the word from the list (A-J) which matches the definition (11-15). There are extra words which you will not need to use (A-J).

An item of clothing worn to keep the feet warm.

11. To be addicted to work.

12. A best-selling song.

13. Having a higher reputation than it deserves.

14. Completely destroyed.

15. Spectacular and wonderful.

A. busy
B. workaholic
C. a virus
D. breathtaking
E. sock
F. overrated
G. ruined
H. a soundtrack
I. a hit single
J. damaged

Finish each sentence (16-20) using a word from the list (A-J). Use each word only once. There are extra words which you will not need to use (A-J).

It hurts my back to sit on this <u>stool</u>. Can we move to a table with chairs?

16. All passengers should collect their _____ before exiting the plane.

17. I am afraid of some insects because they can _____ you.

18. I'm a sales rep. What do you do for a _____?

19. He's a nurse, so sometimes he has to work the night _____.

20. Emma is due to give birth soon, so she has gone on maternity _____.

A. luggage
B. sting
C. job
D. hours
E. break
F. living
G. leave
H. sofa
I. shift
J. stool

Write the word (A-J) that is most often used with a word on the list (21-25) to form a collocation. Use each word only once. There are extra words which you will not need to use (A-J).

Close friend

21. long

22. comfy

23. shiny

24. tasty

25. torrential

A. hours
B. laptop
C. rain
D. building
E. music
F. pillow
G. meal
H. surface
I. outcome
J. friend

WRITING COMPONENT

explanations & tips to maximize your score in the WRITING component!

 The writing component consists of three tasks and lasts for 45 minutes. The level of difficulty of the tasks increases as the test progresses. You will have a paper and pen to make notes.

 TASK 1: SOCIAL NETWORK CHAT

In this part, you are having a social media chat with **another member of a ficticious club** or website you have joined. The theme could be any general English theme.

You will be asked **three questions**, and you need to respond by writing in **informal** English. The word count is 30-40 words. You have 10 minutes to complete the task.

 TASK 2: FORMAL EMAIL RESPONSE

In this part, you have **received an email** regarding feedback, a meeting or a problem you need to complain about.

You need to **respond to the email by writing in formal English** and including the **notes you have been given**. The word count is 120-150 words and you have 15 minutes to complete the task.

 TASK 3: ARTICLE FOR A WEBSITE

In this part, you have to write an **article on a topic of general interest** to send to an online magazine.

You will be given the **topic**, **notes** and **data** to help you with the content. The register is **neutral English**, and it must be informative and interesting to get a high grade. The word count is 180-220 words and you have 20 minutes.

W1: SOCIAL NETWORK CHAT

OVERVIEW

The first task in the writing component is an **informal social network chat**, which takes the form of an interaction with another member of a fictitious club or website you have joined. Examples include: cooking club, travel club, property website, science club.

This task tests your ability to write in an informal and natural way, so in this chapter we will cover the grammatical structures, expressions and punctuation you should use to maximize your score and reach a C1/C2 level.

GRAMMAR HACKS

≫ COMPARISON

You should try to include a comparative or superlative in this task of the writing, but use these more advanced examples rather than the more common forms.

AS... (ADJECTIVE)...AS

- ✅ My friend told me the coastal region is **as** pretty **as** it gets!
- ✅ I hope this club isn't **as** dull **as** the one I used to go to.

DOUBLE COMPARATIVE

- ✅ Since joining the nature club my knowledge of flora and fauna **is getting better and better**.
- ✅ Sadly, the area where I live **is becoming more and more** industrial.

SUPERLATIVES (BY FAR)

- ✅ This is **by far the most** fun group of people I've ever met!
- ✅ This club is **by far the least** expensive one I've seen.

≫ QUESTION TAGS

Adding short tag questions to **ask for agreement** or **check information**, is a simple way of showing the examiner that you are adapting your language to the style of a social network chat, and it makes the interaction seem more authentic.

Just remember to reflect the auxiliary verb (positive to negative/negative to positive) and the subject of the clause, using a comma and a question mark too.

✅ The club **has** been running for years now**, hasn't it?**

✅ They **haven't** decided on the next guest speaker yet**, have they?**

ADVERBS AND CONJUNCTIONS

The style of a social network chat is similar to natural, informal speech so you want to avoid formal conjunctions such as moreover, furthermore or nevertheless as they sound strange in natural spoken English (we'll use these later in task 2).

Adverbs to start your response:

➡ **Well,** the truth is I've never been in a club like this before.

➡ **Actually,** it's the first I've heard about it.

➡ **Sadly,** a lot of the trees in my county have been chopped down in recent years.

➡ **Anyway,** I guess we'll find out next week.

Conjunctions to use in your informal writing and speaking

➡ **That said,** the people seem really nice. (However)

➡ **What's more,** we can get to know each other better. (Moreover)

GET USED TO + ING (TO BE ACCUSTOMED)

This is one of the most common mistakes in exams as students often forget that this expression is followed by + ing. But if you get it right, it's impressive.

✅ I have finally **got used to getting up early** - but it has taken me ages!

✅ I can't seem to **get used to driving everywhere** now that I live so far from town.

GET EXPRESSIONS

As native speakers we probably overuse the word **get**, but **get expressions** in your writing will certainly catch the eye of the examiners and make your writing seem more native.

Here are some of the most impressive examples that you can incorporate into your speaking and writing to maximize your score.

➡ **GET OVER (SOMETHING/SOMEONE) = to accept something from the past and move on**

✅ I felt pretty disappointed when I heard the news, but I guess I'll get over it.

➡️ **GET ON (MY) NERVES** = to irritate and annoy

✅ It really gets on my nerves when people drop litter on the street.

➡️ **GET INVOLVED** = to participate fully in an activity

✅ I've always wanted to get involved in this type of thing.

➡️ **GET ON WITH (SOMETHING)** = to do something without complaining or wasting time

✅ We need to get on with cleaning the garden or we'll never finish on time.

➡️ **GET ALONG WITH (SOMEBODY)** = to have a nice relationship

✅ One of the best things about the club is how well we all get along with each other.

➡️ **GET AWAY** = to escape or have a holiday

✅ We're hoping to get away to the mountains this summer

➤➤ PHRASAL VERBS

Phrasal verbs are used extensively in informal English, so you should try to include a few examples in this writing task.

Remember that if you use a verb **after** a phrasal verb it should be in the +ing (gerund) form as we use this form after prepositions in English.

There are literally thousands of phrasal verbs in English (much to the frustration of language learners) but here are 10 very useful ones to include in your writing:

➡️ **SIGN UP** = to join or register for a course, club or gym.

✅ I decided to sign up for the club as my friend was raving about it.

➡️ **PUT OFF** = to discourage you, or make you change your mind about something

✅ I was going to join a similar club in my town a few years ago, but the fees put me off.

➡️ **COME UP WITH** = to think of an idea, joke, story or invention

✅ I came up with a good idea to raise money for the club.

➡️ **LET (SOMEBODY) DOWN** = to disappoint (somebody)

✅ The club has really let the members down by cancelling the event at such short notice.

➡ **GIVE UP** = to quit or stop doing something

✅ I joined a gym a few years ago, but I gave up due to work commitments.

➡ **JOIN IN** = to become involved in an activity

✅ It's great that our kids can join in the summer events at the club.

➡ **SET UP** = to start or establish a business, school, club or organisation

✅ I heard that the club was set up by a famous writer.

➡ **LOOK UP** = to find information online

✅ I saw a post on Instagram so I decided to look the club up.

➡ **FIND OUT** = to discover information

✅ I only just found out about the monthly events, but I'm pretty keen to get involved.

➡ **TAKE UP** = to start doing an activity or hobby

✅ I recently decided to take up hiking, so this club is perfect for me to get to know fellow hikers.

SOUNDING MORE NATIVE

In this section of the book, you'll learn the more native way to use some common expressions.

›› I LIKE (FOOTBALL) VERY MUCH

This is perfectly understandable, in fact many teachers wouldn't even bother to correct this, but you wouldn't often hear a native English speaker say it, so change it for…

➡ I really like football.

➡ I'm pretty keen on football.

➡ I'm really into football.

›› I DON'T LIKE (FOOTBALL)

English is an indirect language, and we try to soften negative comments if we can by making a positive sentence negative by preceding it with **not** or by using a nice **idiomatic expression**.

➡ I'm not really keen on football.

➡ I'm just not that into football I'm afraid.

➡ Sorry, but football just isn't my cup of tea.

≫ I PRACTISE (SPORTS)

Again, this sounds weird, as the word **practise** in English is reserved for **repeating actions to try to improve**. We play tennis, but we practise our serve (by repeating one aspect of the game to try to improve it).

 PLAY = for sports with a ball, puck or shuttlecock (hockey, basketball, tennis)

 GO = for sports that involve movement from A to B (swimming, jogging, cycling)

 DO = for sports without a ball and in a gym (yoga, aerobics, karate, crossfit)

≫ THE PRINCIPAL PROBLEM

This isn't technically incorrect, but it's more natural to use **main** instead of principal in English. So use the main problem, or better still the main issue.

≫ "HOW ARE YOU?" "I'M FINE, THANK YOU."

Okay, so you've been taught this response verbatim in every English class you had at school and it has stuck. But honestly, if you ask an English person "How are you?" they are much more likely to respond with either:

➡ I'm great, thanks!

➡ I'm really well, thank you.

➡ Not bad, thanks.

If my British friend responded with "I'm fine, thank you." I'd think that either they were having problems they didn't want to discuss at the time, or that they were in a bad mood with me!

≫ I WANT THAT THEY TEACH ME TO SPEAK LIKE A NATIVE

This is a clear translation from Latin languages that have a subjunctive, but it sounds strange in English. Instead we would say:

➡ I want them to teach me to speak like a native.

≫ I THINK...

This is probably one of the most overused words in English exams, for the simple reason that you are being asked your opinion on many topics. It sounds so much better to use these expressions:

➡ I reckon... (informal)
➡ I guess... (informal)
➡ I imagine... (neutral)
➡ I suppose... (neutral)

PUNCTUATION

As this is a chat, you should use informal punctuation to make it seem more natural.

≫ CONTRACTIONS

In task 1 of the writing component you should contract all the words to their short forms:

If I had known, I would have joined earlier. ➡ If I'd known, I'd have joined earlier.

≫ A DASH

In informal writing we can add a dash to add emphasis. The dash is used in place of a colon and we can also add an exclamation mark at the end.

The team spirit, helping the environment and being outdoors - this is what attracted me to the club!

≫ EXCLAMATION MARKS

You can add these to your writing too - just don't overuse them as it seems messy and childish. We would recommend no more than two in this task.

W1: SOCIAL NETWORK CHAT

 In this part you will chat to a member in a social network chat.
You should write 30-40 words.
You have a maximum of 10 minutes on this task in the exam, but you should try and complete it in 5 minutes to leave more time for task 3!

 Watch the quick tutorial video for this part of the writing exam for tips, strategies, expressions and model answers.

STEP 1: READ THE TASK CAREFULLY

You are a new member of a nature club.
You are chatting to another member in the online club chat room.
Respond to the messages in full sentences.
Write 30-40 words per response.

©aptisacademy.com

STEP 2: BRAINSTORM TOPIC VOCABULARY

countryside	species	picturesque	relax
coastline	flowers	natural	calm down
mountains	bees	breathtaking	protect
lakes	flora and fauna	endangered	appreciate
forest	butterflies	gorgeous	

©aptisacademy.com

STEP 3: USE A RANGE OF GRAMMAR

Comparatives
Superlatives
A range of different tenses (not just present simple!)
Used to (past habits and states)
Conditionals

©aptisacademy.com

STEP 4: USE A RANGE OF VOCABULARY

Tag questions (isn't it?)
Get expressions (Get to know new people)
Adverbs (Well, actually, personally)
Phrasal verbs (take off, put up with)

©aptisacademy.com

STEP 5: USE A RANGE OF PUNCTUATION

Question marks (?)
Exclamation marks (!)
commas (,)
Contractions (don't, haven't, wouldn't)

©aptisacademy.com

Hello, I see that you have recently joined our club. I've been a member since I moved out of the city as now I have a big garden. Mind sharing why you have joined the club?

Hi there, thanks for your message. Yes, I have recently joined as I want to know more about the beautiful areas in my country. I just love learning about all the flora and fauna in the region too.

(37 words)

What have you learned so far? What's the most beautiful place in your country?

Well, I've learned about the different species of trees in the north of my country, and now I can identify them easily. There are many gorgeous places in Scotland, but I guess I love the picturesque eastern coastline the most.

(40 words)

That's sounds lovely. Have you heard that the club is going to invite guest speakers to come and talk about different nature-related topics? What do you think of the idea?

Actually, it's a great idea as we can learn so much from experts. I wouldn't mind seeing a presentation on insects such as bees or butterflies. I only hope the lectures are more interactive than in my previous club!

(40 words)

Outdoor Club

 You are a new member of an outdoor club. You are chatting to another member in the online club chat room. Write 30-40 words per response.

Hi, I see that you have recently joined our club. I've been a member for the past few years. Why have you decided to join the club?

What kind of outdoor activities do you enjoy?

That is pretty impressive! Our club has suggested doing a three-day rafting and hiking trip, would you be interested in going?

Environmental Club

You are a new member of an environmental club. You are chatting to another member in the online club chat room. Write 30-40 words per response.

Hi, I see that you have recently joined our club. I've been a member for the past few years. Why have you decided to join the club?

What do you think we need to do to help our planet?

Our club has suggested organising regular visits to some local beaches to pick up rubbish, would you be interested in helping?

>> You are a new member of a history club. You are chatting to another member in the online club chat room. Write 30-40 words per response.

> Hello, I see that you have recently joined our club.
> I've been a member for almost a month. Why have you joined the club?

> Which period of history are you most interested in?

> Our club has suggested organising tours of the local landmarks.
> What do you think of the idea?

Music Club

>> You are a new member of a music club. You are chatting to another member in the online club chat room. Write 30-40 words per response.

Hello fellow music fan. I've been a member of this club since I moved to the city centre. Mind sharing why you have joined?

What kind of concerts do you like going to?

Some other members suggested organising jamming sessions for any musicians in the group to play together. What do you think?

W2: FORMAL EMAIL RESPONSE

OVERVIEW

The second task in the writing component is a **formal email reponse** to an email you have received. Examples include school meeting, airline complaint and hotel feedback.

This task tests your ability to write in a formal and polite manner, so in this chapter we will cover the grammatical structures, organization, expressions and punctuation you should use to maximize your score and reach a C1/C2 level.

GRAMMAR HACKS

≫ THE PASSIVE VOICE

We use the passive voice in formal English to **make criticisms and complaints seem less direct** and so as not to attack the person directly.

This ability to criticise, but be polite, is one of the subtle differences between a C1 and C2 level response.

❌ **You have made** several mistakes regarding my account. (Too direct/personal)

✅ It appears that several mistakes **have been made** regarding my account.

❌ If **you need proof**, I have a copy of the signed contract. (Too direct/personal)

✅ If **proof is needed**, I have a copy of the signed contract.

≫ CONDITIONAL (2nd & 3rd)

In all English tests, conditionals are regarded as **advanced grammatical structures** so we recommend incorporating an example. As **second** and **third conditional** are the most complicated in structure, try to use them if you can.

➡ **IF + PAST SIMPLE, WOULD + INFINITIVE (2ND)**

✅ **If** it **were** necessary, I **would not hesitate** to contract the services of a lawyer.

➡ **IF + PAST PERFECT, WOULD + PRESENT PERFECT (3RD)**

✅ **If** I **had not opened** my email, I **would have been** subjected to unjustified legal action.

⟫ CONJUNCTIONS

As this is an example of formal writing, we should be using **formal conjunctions**. Apart from the usual (however, although) we could take the opportunity to use these more impressive examples:

➡ **NEVERITHELESS/ALBEIT**

✅ It has been a minor **nevertheless** inconvenient error.

✅ It has been a minor **albeit** inconvenient error.

➡ **MOREOVER/FURTHERMORE**

✅ **Moreover**, this is the first correspondence I have received regarding this matter.

✅ **Furthermore**, this is the first correspondence I have received regarding this matter.

➡ **UNLIKE**

✅ **Unlike** my previous bank, RAB bank has always offered me a good service.

➡ **DESPITE (+ING/NOUN)**

✅ **Despite being** a loyal customer, I find myself in an unfavourable legal dispute.

✅ **Despite my loyal custom**, I find myself in an unfavourable legal dispute.

➡ **WHEREAS**

✅ I have always made my repayments on time, **whereas** RAB bank has made my instalments late.

⟫ MODAL VERBS

If you need to ask a question in this task it's recommendable to use a **modal verb** to make it sound more **polite**.

❓ **May** I ask you to recheck my account before taking any further action?
❓ **Could** I ask if this has been taken into account?

⟫ GERUND AS A SUBJECT

Using a gerund (+ ing form of a verb) as the subject of a sentence is another of those **advanced grammatical structures** favoured by examiners.

✅ **Having** been a loyal customer for several years, I am disappointed with this situation.
✅ **Being** a bank clerk myself, I was rather surprised to receive this correspondence.

PUNCTUATION

As this task needs to be in a formal style, you should use more formal punctuation than in task 1.

⟫ NO CONTRACTIONS

In this task, you should use the **full form** of the words

❌ If I'd known, I'd have contacted the bank directly.

✅ If I had known, I would have contacted the bank directly.

⟫ COLONS (:)

Colons can be used to present an **explanation**, draw **attention** to something or **join ideas** together.

- There are several basic services that a bank should offer: **loans, accounts and mortgages.**
- My bank must give me the best service possible: **security and excellent customer service.**

⟫ ETC.

Try and avoid overusing **etc.** in English exams as it gives the impression that you can't be bothered to think of any more examples.

Instead, use among others or and so on as both these phrases can be used at the end of a list to indicate that there might be other examples too.

- This includes accounts, mortgages and loans, **among others.**
- This includes accounts, mortgages and loans, **and so on.**

BEING MORE NATIVE

⟫ DON'T BE VERBOSE

In the romantic languages (French, Spanish, Italian and so on) there is a tendency to write long sentences as they are deemed to be more 'academic' or 'formal'. This is **not the case in the English** language, which favours being **succinct** and not wasting words.

Many students write overly-long sentences in the belief that this is more 'advanced', but it just leads to grammatical errors and a lack of clarity.

We often use short sentences in English to be emphatic or to illustrate a point, so you can use a variety of longer and shorter sentences in your English writing.

⟫ EMAIL FIXED EXPRESSIONS

The model answers on the platform contain the natural expressions we use as native speakers to start an email, complain, emphasise a point and to sign off. As these are the actual phrases we use in **genuine correspondence**, don't be afraid to use them word for word in this particular task.

⟫ UPGRADE YOUR QUANTIFIERS

In spoken English, we would use phrases like **a lot of** and **loads of** to quantify nouns.
As this is formal communication we should use **several** or **a significant amount of** instead.

❌ I have received **a lot of** emails from the bank. (Too informal)

✅ I have received **several** emails from the bank.

❌ I have wasted **loads of** time. (Too informal)

✅ I have wasted a **significant amount** of time.

⟫ AVOID PHRASAL VERBS & 'GET' EXPRESSIONS

You'll be happy to know that formal written English vocabulary is **more similar to Latin languages.** For this reason, you can forget about phrasal verbs and get expressions in this task and choose the Latin-based vocabulary translation instead.

❌ I **handed in** all my papers on time. (Too informal)

✅ I **presented** all my papers on time.

❌ I **got** angry when I read the fine print. (Too informal)

✅ I **became** rather angry when I read the fine print.

⟫ RATHER & SOMEWHAT (QUITE)

To be polite in English we often put **adverbs** before **negative adjectives** to soften the meaning and make the criticism less direct.

- I feel that this is **rather** unprofessional on the part of RAB Bank.
- I feel that this is **somewhat** unprofessional on the part of RAB Bank.

THE APTIS ACADEMY GUIDE TO

FORMAL EMAILS

1. GREET THE PERSON

Dear Sir or Madam,

Dear Customer Services,

2. WHY ARE YOU WRITING?

I am contacting you regarding your recent email.

I feel compelled to write to you regarding...

*mention your feelings in this paragraph

3. THREE PARAGRAPHS

First of all...
Another point is...
Last, but by no means least,...

CONJUNCTIONS
Moreover,...
Additionally,...
Furthermore,...
In consequence,...

4. NEED TO COMPLAIN?

The... has not been up to the expected standard.

I am bitterly disappointed with the...

(E.g. customer service)

5. MAKE A SUGGESTION

I strongly recommend that your organisation...

May I suggest... (+ing)

It would be advisable to...

6. ASK A QUESTION

May I ask if...?

Would you be so kind as to tell me if...?

Has this been taken into consideration?

6. FINAL SENTENCE

I look forward to receiving your reply.

I would appreciate a prompt reply to this email.

I hope my suggestions will be taken into account in my absence.

7. SIGN OFF

Yours faithfully,
Mr T Briggs
(If you're writing to a department and don't have a name)

Yours sincerely,
Mr T Briggs
(If you are writing to a specific person)

W2: FORMAL EMAIL RESPONSE

In this part you will read an email and write a response.
You need to respond to the email in 120-150 words by using the notes provided and expressing how you feel about the situation.
You should spend a <u>maximum of 15 minutes</u> on this task in the exam.

 Watch the quick tutorial video for this part of the writing exam for tips from the authors and model answers.

THREE TYPES OF EMAIL

COMPLAINT   FEEDBACK   MEETING

AREAS YOU WILL BE SCORED ON

1 STRUCTURE
Divide your response into 5 paragraphs with a formal opening and closing statement.

3 CONTENT
Include all 3 points from the notes and develop them to form a paragraph for each point.

2 STYLE
Write in a formal style (no contractions, informal expressions, phrasal verbs etc).

4 LANGUAGE
Use a range of vocabulary, grammatical structures and cohesive devices.

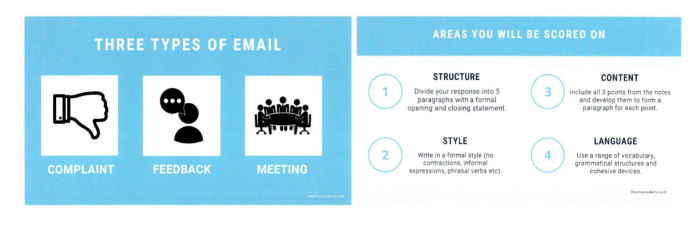

BANK EMAIL

Dear Customer,

I am writing to request the immediate repayment of your outstanding loan to the amount of €500 (1). As outlined in your loan agreement, this amount was lent to you on the condition that it be repaid at the end of the calendar month (2). This is the third occasion on which we have contacted you regarding this matter, but to date we have received no response (3).

If you do not repay the full amount within 3 working days, we will have no option but to suspend your account and pass your case onto our legal department, which could result in legal proceedings.

Yours faithfully,
RAB Bank LTD

Your notes:
(1) Not €500, but €300 – got contract to prove it
(2) Agreement for end of year, not month – spoke with manager by phone about it
(3) Not true!! – first contact I´ve had about this!

 The first style of email we are going to look at is a complaint email. All three email styles use a **similar structure**, but the **tone of your writing will change** depending on whether it's a complaint email, feedback email or meeting email.

Divide your email into clear paragraphs with a space between

Be polite and indirect with your complaints

Link your paragraphs together coherently

Use advanced conjunctions within paragraphs to connect sentences

Use fixed 'complaining' expressions

Request that they take action

Finish strong, but be polite

Dear Loan Services,

I am contacting you regarding your recent email as <u>I am afraid that</u> there appear to be several errors in your system.

<u>First and foremost,</u>the amount was €300 as opposed to €500. If proof is needed I have my copy of the signed contract.

<u>Another point is that</u> in my recent telephone conversation with the manager it was agreed that the loan be repaid by the end of the year.

<u>Last, but by no means least</u>, I have not received any prior correspondence regarding this matter; <u>therefore</u> it seems unfair to me that the bank appears to have changed the repayment terms without warning.

<u>The customer service I have received regarding this issue has not been up to the expected standard.</u>

<u>May I request that you recheck my account before taking this matter any further?</u>

<u>I would appreciate a prompt reply to this letter.</u>

Yours faithfully,
Ms. Brown

 Think carefully about the **tone** of your email before you start writing. In this example, the bank is threatening to take unjustified legal action, so **you might feel angry and worried** about the situation and this would be reflected in your choice of expressions.

 This example is a clear **C2 response** and yours doesn't have to be this perfect to score a C1. That said, there are a lot of fixed expressions here that you can use in your own writing, as this is how we really write in English.

 Don't be tempted to write more than the word count in this task - it won't do you any favours with the examiners and you need to complete this in a <u>maximum of 15 minutes</u> to leave enough time for the article.

ONLINE SHOPPING

You recently bought a fridge from an online electronics company and you are not satisfied with your purchase.

Write an email to the customer services department including the notes below.

My notes:
(1) Old model not new one in the photograph
(2) Delivery man didn't call – delivered next door, too heavy to move
(3) Credit card **charged** twice – need refund

 Sometimes you may receive a **notice with instructions** and your notes as in the example above. However, the structure remains the same: **3 points = three paragraphs.**

 The notes are often **deliberately informal** (and are not full sentences) which forces you to paraphrase them to transform the same idea into **formal** language.

 Use the model answer from the previous page to help you to construct your response. Remember that you must include ALL the notes to score a C1/C2 level in this task.

STYLE 2: FEEDBACK EMAIL

SUPERMARKET FEEDBACK

Dear Customer,

In an attempt to improve our facilities and offer a better service to our customers, we are requesting feedback from our most valued clients.

We would appreciate your feedback on our store layout (1), our in-store music (2) and our customer service (3).

Many thanks for your collaboration.

Kind regards,
The Management

My notes:
(1) Products organised illogically
(2) Music annoying!
(3) Huge lines at checkout

 For a feedback email you should use exactly the **same structure** as for a complaint email, but your **tone should be more gentle**. After all, they have called you a 'valued client' and they are making an effort to improve their service to please you. 🙂

 We recommend **complimenting them on something they do well, mentioning the problem and then making a suggestion on how to improve**. Your paragraph might read something like this:

Although the supermarket has an admirable range of products, it is often difficult to locate a specific item. May I suggest reorganising your products and aisles in a more logical manner?

FEEDBACK EMAIL PRACTICE

Dear Customer,

GYM FEEDBACK

In an attempt to improve our facilities and offer a better service to clients we are requesting feedback from our customers.

As a valued customer, we would appreciate your feedback on our (1) staff, (2) equipment and (3) opening hours.

Many thanks for your collaboration.

Kind regards,
The Management

My notes:
(1) Unfriendly staff
(2) Outdated machines
(3) Not good enough!

After you have written your responses, check them against the model answers (C2 level) on our e-learning platform, then write an improved version yourself.

STYLE 3: MEETING EMAIL

Dear Parent,

SCHOOL MEETING

You are invited to attend our upcoming school meeting which will take place next Monday in the school hall. We will be discussing a number of changes within the school, including changing the school menu to vegetarian (1), implementing an e-learning platform (2) and the end of year trip (3).

Please advise if you will be able to attend or not. We are looking forward to your response.

Kind regards,
The Principal

My notes:
(1) Healthier?
(2) Great idea, but expensive/user-friendly?
(3) Cultural trip instead of beach holiday?

 Again, here you are going to use the **same structure** we have been using in previous emails, but in this situation **you want your opinions and questions to be taken into account** - although you cannot attend the meeting in person.

 We recommend **mentioning something positive about the point, then raising a question** about it (the same question you might have asked if you had been able to attend the meeting).

Your paragraph structure might read like this:

First and foremost, I fully support the need to update the children's menu. May I ask if the school intends to improve the nutritional value of the meals on offer at the same time?

MEETING EMAIL PRACTICE

Dear Resident,

LOCAL COUNCIL MEETING

You are invited to attend our upcoming council meeting which will take place on Monday the 5th in the Old Mill Hotel on William's Street, at 7pm.

We will be discussing a number of points at the meeting, including the construction of the new shopping centre (1), necessary road works next month (2) and using LED bulbs in our street lighting (3).

Please advise if you will be able to attend or not. We are looking forward to your response.

Kind regards,
The Secretary

My notes:
(1) Enough parking?!
(2) Timetable of disruption?
(3) Good!, but sounds pricey

After you have written your responses, check them against the model answers (C2 level) on our e-learning platform, then write an improved version yourself.

W3: ARTICLE FOR A WEBSITE

OVERVIEW

The final task of the writing component is an **article for website publication**. The article must be both **informative** and **interesting** to reach a C1/C2 grade. Examples include articles on topics such as the environment, new technologies, health, travel and the economy.

This task tests your ability to write in an **engaging** way, using **advanced English expressions, phrases and idioms.** This is clearly the most challenging writing task in the test, so in this chapter we are going to study the structures, vocabulary, grammar and punctuation you should use to maximize your score.

GRAMMAR HACKS

➤➤ CONJUNCTIONS

In addition to the conjunctions we have already covered in previous chapters. Here we will cover some elegant C2 level examples for you to study.

➡️ **HAVING SAID THAT**

✅ Year by year, humans are encroaching on the natural habitats of endangered species. **Having said that**, there are a few notable success stories in Africa.

➡️ **AS A CONSEQUENCE**

✅ NGOs around the world are working hard to fight back. **As a consequence**, certain species are making a comeback.

➡️ **NONETHELESS (NEVERTHELESS)**

✅ It has been a difficult, **nonetheless** important fight.

➡️ **INDEED (USED FOR EMPHASIS/TO CONFIRM A PREVIOUS STATEMENT)**

✅ Greenpeace has long fought for our planet. **Indeed**, it was the first organisation of its kind.

➡️ **YET (ALTHOUGH)**

✅ We have made great progress in raising awareness, **yet** there is still room for improvement.

➡️ **NEITHER…NOR**

✅ Many humans are **neither** aware of the plight of many species **nor** willing to make small changes in their lives to protect the environment.

➤➤ VERB INVERSIONS

The most common use of the verb inversion in English is when asking questions. It simply means we need to put the verb/auxiliary verb before the subject (When are you arriving?) (Do you want to come?). However, there are several high-level **negative adverbs and adverb phrases** that you need to follow with a verb inversion. Here we will cover the most useful ones for this section of the writing.

➡️ **RARELY/SELDOM**

✅ **Rarely** in human history have we seen such devastation.

✅ **Seldom** do we stop to think about the consequences of our actions.

➡️ **ONLY THEN**

✅ **Only then** will we realise the precious gift we have been given by the cosmos.

➡️ **ON NO ACCOUNT**

✅ **On no account** should we forget the fragility of the planet we live on.

➤➤ RHETORICAL QUESTIONS

A rhetorical question is not really a question at all – as it doesn't require a response. They are used extensively in presentations as a way of **sequencing ideas together and engaging the audience in thought.** For this reason, they are a useful way of engaging your reader in an article.

They can be used effectively in the **opening paragraph to capture attention**, as well as to start a paragraph before going on to answer the question yourself in the following sentences.

✅ What are the consequences of these actions?

✅ Will humans ever take responsibility for their actions?

VOCABULARY

➤➤ IDIOMATIC EXPRESSIONS

Using idiomatic expressions correctly in your article shows a **proficient level** of English. There are thousands of idioms in the English language, but here are 10 useful ones with meanings that could be cleverly incorporated into your article – whatever the topic.

➡️ **THE BALL IS IN YOUR COURT** (It's up to you to make the next decision or take the next step)

✅ Will humans act in time to save endangered species from extinction? The ball is in your court.

➡️ **ACTIONS SPEAK LOUDER THAN WORDS** (You are judged on what you do, not what you say.)

✅ Many people show regret when they hear about the plight of the African elephant, but actions speak louder than words, and we need to act now.

➡️ **A HOT POTATO** (A disputed issue that nobody wants to deal with)

✅ The trafficking of endangered species has become a political hot potato in Asia.

➡️ **EVERY CLOUD HAS A SILVER LINING** (There is always good hidden in something bad)

✅ The photo of the massacred elephant was horrific to see, but every cloud has a silver lining and the shocking images spurred many organisations into decisive action to save these magnificent beasts.

➡️ **COST AN ARM AND A LEG** (To be expensive)

✅ Contributing to this cause doesn't have to cost an arm and a leg. Much can be done at grassroots level to fight the destruction.

➡️ **SIT ON THE FENCE** (To not make a decision or not choose sides in a disagreement)

✅ We must not sit on the fence about this issue. We must pull together and make lasting changes to the way we interact with our environment.

➡️ **CROSS THAT BRIDGE WHEN YOU COME TO IT** (To deal with a problem only if it happens)

✅ This is not a simple case of crossing that bridge when we come to it; we need to plan for the future or it could be too late.

➡️ **CUT CORNERS** (To do something badly to try to save time or money)

✅ Environmental protection needs huge investments of time and money. We simply cannot cut corners.

➡️ **TO KILL TWO BIRDS WITH ONE STONE** (To accomplish two different things with the same action)

✅ We have a chance here to kill two birds with one stone. We can raise both money and awareness for this worthwhile cause.

➡️ **THE LAST STRAW** (The final bad thing, after a series of bad things)

✅ Aside from the destruction of their natural habits and global warming, poaching could be the last straw for the majestic elephant.

⟫ PROVERBS

Proverbs are **valuable wisdom** passed on through the ages and English has many! So, here's a list of 8 particularly astute ones that you should learn and try to use in your writing.

➡ A JOURNEY OF A THOUSAND MILES BEGINS WITH A SIMPLE STEP

You must begin something if you hope to finish it; something that takes a long time to finish begins with one step.

➡ A PICTURE IS WORTH A THOUSAND WORDS

An image can tell a story better than words can.

➡ HOPE FOR THE BEST, PREPARE FOR THE WORST

In any situation, be optimistic about the result, but always be ready for the worst outcome.

➡ THE GRASS IS ALWAYS GREENER ON THE OTHER SIDE

People always want what others have; they always think someone else's life is better.

➡ THE PEN IS MIGHTIER THAN THE SWORD

If you're trying to convince someone of something, words and ideas are stronger than using physical force (common in politics).

➡ WHEN THE GOING GETS TOUGH, THE TOUGH GET GOING

When a situation becomes difficult, strong people don't give up; they work harder

➡ YOU CAN LEAD A HORSE TO WATER, BUT YOU CAN'T MAKE IT DRINK

You can try to help someone by giving good advice, but you can't force them to follow it.

➡ TWO HEADS ARE BETTER THAN ONE

It's easier to do something as a team than all by yourself.

In this part, you will write an article for a website which is informative and interesting. You will be given notes and data on which to base your article. The article needs to be between 180 - 220 words.
You should spend about 20 minutes on this task in the test.

Watch the quick tutorial video for this part of the writing exam for tips and strategies from the authors.

You will write an article on a topic of general interest, which you need to write in an informative and interesting style.

You need to base your article on the notes given, but you do not need to include all the notes. The key is to select the most interesting or surprising data and develop the ideas in order to send a message to your reader.

Your article should be between 180 –220 words, but you should write close to the maximum word count to receive a high score.

Although there are two styles of article (notes + data, complex data) you can use a similar structure - with a few adjustments.

©aptisacademy.com

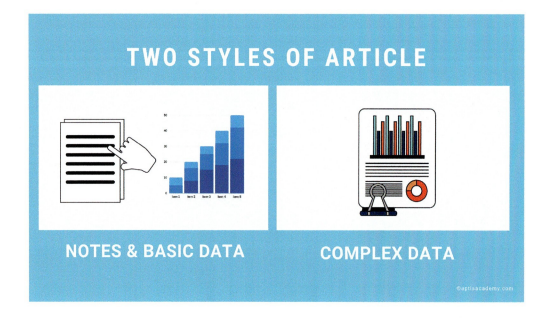

TWO STYLES OF ARTICLE

NOTES & BASIC DATA

COMPLEX DATA

©aptisacademy.com

STRUCTURE

1 Divide your response into 5 paragraphs, with an opening paragraph and a final thought.

CONTENT

3 Base your article on the notes, but use your own words and ideas to develop the content.

STYLE

2 Write in a lively and engaging style, using neutral English (not too informal or too formal).

LANGUAGE

4 Use a range of collocations, expressions, grammatical structures and cohesive devices.

©aptisacademy.com

ARTICLE STYLE 1: NOTES & BASIC DATA

Endangered Species & Conservation

Quite Interesting (QI.com) is a website that welcomes articles from readers on topics of general interest. You have decided to submit an article on the topic of **endangered species and conservation**.

You have done some research and produced a diagram. Using your information and notes, write an interesting and informative article to send to the website. Write between 180-220 words.

My notes:

- More than 2,000 endangered species worldwide (panda, elephant, rhino)
- Many species may be extinct in 10-15 years
- Global actions: fight illegal hunting, develop sustainable tourism
- Individual actions: volunteer to raise money, sign global petitions

Endangered Species Research

	1900	1950	2000
African Elephant	Over 1 million	250,000	45,000
Bengal Tiger	500,000	85,000	78,000
Bornean Orang-utan	350,000	300,000	67,000

PLANNING YOUR ARTICLE: STYLE 1

If you want to score highly on this task, it's absolutely vital that you take the time to **plan your structure, paragraph content and organization**. You should leave <u>20 minutes</u> for this task in the test: 5 minutes for planning, and 15 minutes for writing, proofreading and editing.

In the next few pages we're going to show you the paragraph structure we recommend and how we would plan the content of each paragraph for this example task.

- Start your article with a **general sentence** to introduce the importance of this topic in the world today.
- **Choose** which of the **notes** you can use here. We have chosen the first two points from the notes as they support the severity of the situation.
- End the paragraph with a **rhetorical question** to your reader. This question will be referred to again in the closing paragraph (P5) to link your article together.
- **3 sentences** would be ideal for P1.

- Use the second paragraph to neatly **summarize the data** included in the table.
- Focus on the **key changes** or **trends** in the data by asking yourself these questions:

1. **What is the time-frame of the data?** Can you express this without repeating the years?
2. **What is the most significant change?** Quote the statistics here.
3. **Do the other animals follow the same trend or is it different?** Are they all increasing or decreasing in number?
- **3 or 4 sentences** would be ideal for P2.

- Divide the rest of the notes into two logical paragraphs. In this case **global actions (P3)** and **individual actions (P4)**.

- Brainstorm **your own ideas** around the point then develop them into **2 paragraphs**:

Fight illegal hunting 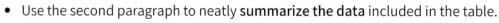 poaching/hunters/massacre/ivory tusks/Africa/illegal trade.
Develop sustainable tourism ➡ eco-tourism/protect eco-systems/limit numbers.

Volunteer to raise money ➡ fundraising for charity/sponsorship/collections
Sign global petitions ➡ social media/NGOs/activism/awareness

- **3 sentences** for **each paragraph** (P3 & P4) would be ideal.

- End your article by first **referring to the rhetorical question** you asked in P1 and then **answering the question in a few words.**
- End your article with a sentence about **what the future will be like** if nothing changes. A **first conditional sentence** would be perfect here.
- **3 sentences** in this final paragraph would be ideal.

Include a title by using your rhetorical question from P1.

This is an opening sentence structure you could use.

Here are the notes we chose to include.

Endangered Species: Is it too late?

Not a day goes by without stories of endangered creatures appearing in the news. The WWF states that there are over 2,000 animals on the endangered species list and it is predicted that many may be extinct within the next two decades. What can be done to stop this? Or is it simply too late?

Here's our rheorical question.

Here we have summarized the data from the table.

Recent research has revealed shocking data regarding the plight of some of the most iconic creatures on planet Earth. Over the past century, the number of African Elephants has plummeted from over 1 million individuals, to merely 34,000. Sadly, the numbers of tigers and orang-utans have shown a similar decline.

Here we are using another question to introduce the paragraph about global actions (P3).

What can be done at the global level to reverse these trends? Efforts should be made to clamp down on illegal poaching, particularly on the African continent where elephants and rhinos are massacred for their ivory tusks. Tourism to such biodiverse areas should be limited, and visitors encouraged to 'shoot with your camera, not with a gun'.

P4 discusses our ideas for individual actions.

If governments are too weak to fight the illegal ivory trade then we must take action at the individual level. We can raise awareness by signing and sharing petitions on social media, pressuring politicians to act. We can support NGOs through charitable donations and sponsored fun runs. The options are endless.

P5 is our final message to our reader referring to our original rhetorical question.

In a nutshell, action must be taken now at both the global and individual level. It is not too late, but we must act now or future generations will only see these creatures in storybooks.

There is no doubt that this is the most challenging task in the test. But by following our advice about **planning**, **structure**, **content**, **cohesion** and **editing** you can get a high score.

This example is a clear **C2 response** and yours doesn't have to be this perfect to score a C1. That said, there are a lot of suggestions here that you can use in your own writing to link your paragraphs together and send a clear message to your reader.

When you have finished writing it's very important to **edit your work**. You could write a really good article, then lose points for careless misspellings and receive a lower level than you deserve. This would be such a pity, so always edit your work!

Technology Use & Children's Health

Quite Interesting (QI.com) is a website that welcomes articles from readers on topics of general interest. You have decided to submit an article on the topic of **technology use and children's health.**

You have done some research and produced a diagram. Using your information and notes, write an interesting and informative article to send to the website. Write between 180-220 words.

My notes:
- Direct correlation between poor eyesight and screen time.
- Advantages such as social, critical thinking and ability to solve problems.

Research: Children's Eyesight

	2000	2020	2050 (predicted)
% of children wearing glasses globally	30.4%	38.4%	50.1%

 Use the paragraph planning to constuct your article before you start writing. Don't pay any attention to timing at the moment, just focus on producing an article by planning your content and using the grammar and vocabulary hacks from this chapter.

 The theme of **new technologies** is a common one in the test, whether it be in the speaking, listening, reading or writing component. It would be a good idea to think about **the pros and cons of new technologies in the modern world** before your test so you're well-prepared.

 After you have written your responses, check them against the model answers (C2 level) on our e-learning platform then write an improved version yourself.

aptis academy**.com**

The Olympic Games

Quite Interesting (QI.com) is a website that welcomes articles from readers on topics of general interest. You have decided to submit an article on the topic of **the Olympic Games.**

You have done some research and produced a diagram. Using your information and notes, write an interesting and informative article to send to the website. Write between 180-220 words.

My notes:

- Advantages: international prestige, encourages kids into sport
- Disadvantages: expensive, installations abandoned after the event

Research: The Olympics

	Budget	Final Cost
Athens, Greece (2004)	$8 billion	$11 billion
Beijing, China (2008)	$10 billion	$30 billion
Sochi, Russia (2014)	$10 billion	$50 billion

Source: Forbes business

Now you have practised planning your article (and studied the model answers) we recommend that you try to complete this practice article in 20 minutes: 5 to plan, 15 to write and edit.

After you have written your responses, check them against the model answers (C2 level) on our e-learning platform then write an improved version yourself.

Quality of Life

Quite Interesting (QI.com) is a website that welcomes articles from readers on topics of general interest. You have decided to submit an article on the topic of **the quality of life in three cities.**

You have done some research and produced a diagram. Using your information and notes, write an interesting and informative article to send to the website. Write between 180-220 words.

Research: Three Cities

	Availability of Housing	Unemployment rate	Safety
Zurich, Switzerland	3rd	3rd	1st
Auckland, New Zealand	2nd	1st	2nd
Vancouver, Canada	1st	2nd	3rd

PLANNING YOUR ARTICLE: STYLE 2

The first thing you will notice here is that rather than having some written notes to include along with some basic data, we have no notes to help us but the data is more detailed. On some occasions, the task might include some simple notes, but it's clear that the information in the table needs to be **discussed in more detail.**

In the test, you will have to decide quickly on which structure is the best to use, so ask yourself a simple question: **Could I summarise the data into one paragraph? Or is there too much information contained in it?**

In this case, we can see that we couldn't possibly inform our reader about all the points included in the data in one small paragraph, so we're going to have to write a paragraph about each of the cities separately.

In the next few pages, we're going to show you the paragraph structure we recommend and how we would plan the content of each paragraph for this example task.

There is always the chance that you genuinely don't know anything at all about the cities mentioned - maybe you've never even heard of them!

The important thing to remember in this task, and indeed all tasks in the writing and speaking component, is that the truth is completely irrelevant.

It doesn't matter if what you say is true in real life or completely invented. There is no section of the marking scales for 'truth' so feel free to say whatever you like. It's the **message**, **structure**, **vocabulary**, **grammar content** and **cohesion** that really count.

- Start your article with a **general sentence** to introduce the topic to your reader.
- End the 1st paragraph with a **rhetorical question** to your reader. This question will be referred to again in the closing paragraph (P5) to link your article together.
- **2 sentences** would be ideal for P1.

- Use the second paragraph to introduce the subjects of your research. In this case you just need to mention the fact that the research was done on three cities and what the criteria was.
- **2 sentences** would be ideal for P2.

- Now you are going to write **3 paragraphs** and focus on the characteristics of each city in each paragraph. P3 (Zurich) P4 (Auckland) P5 (Vancouver).
- Ask yourself what are the best features of each city and speculate about the impact of this on the **quality of life** there.
- **3 sentences** would be ideal for **each of the paragraphs** (P3, P4 & P5)

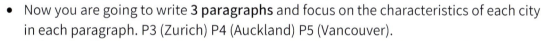

- End your article by first **referring to the rhetorical question** you asked in P1 and **answer** the question in a few words.
- Then speak to the reader personally and end with a final comment.
- **2/3 sentences** would be ideal for P6.

 Notice that you have **6 paragraphs** in this style of article, but that the paragraphs are shorter.

STYLE 2: MODEL ANSWER

Here we have written a clever title by making a proverb into a question.

You could start with a question to engage your reader in the first 2 sentences.

Here we introduce the research and the criteria it includes.

Here are the benefits of the economy and housing for citizens.

Our final message to our reader is that any of these cities could be a good option for them personally.

Now we use one paragraph for each city.

Notice how we are interpreting the data, not saying 1st, 2nd, 3rd - which would be repetitive.

Where is the grass always greener?

Are you thinking about moving to a new city? If so, then you should consider one of these amazing places.

New research has named Zurich, Auckland and Vancouver within the top 10 best cities to live in the world. Some of the criteria include housing, jobs and safety.

Take Vancouver, a bustling coastal city in Canada. It boasts a booming economy alongside a massive array of house and flats to rent or buy. Settling down here would be a great move for anyone, as finding your dream home would be a piece of cake.

What about setting up home in Zurich? It prides itself on being one of the safest places to live in the world. Crime rates are exceptionally low all over Switzerland, meaning the population lives with peace of mind - which is priceless if you have a family.

And not forgetting Auckland, a major city on the north island of New Zealand and home to one of the tallest buildings in the southern hemisphere. It's got one of the lowest rates of unemployment in the world, making it an ideal place for job hunters wanting to move up the career ladder.

In a nutshell, any of these cities would be a superb place to live and would live up to even the highest expectations.

There is no doubt that this is the most challenging task in the test. But by following our advice about **planning**, **structure**, **content**, **cohesion** and **editing** you can get a high score.

This example is a clear **C2 response** and yours doesn't have to be this perfect to score a C1. That said, there are a lot of suggestions here that you can use in your own writing to link your paragraphs together and send a clear message to your reader.

When you have finished writing it's very important to **edit your work**. You could write a really good article, then lose points for careless misspellings and receive a lower level than you deserve. This would be such a pity, so always edit your work!

Types of Travel

Quite Interesting (QI.com) is a website that welcomes articles from readers on topics of general interest. You have decided to submit an article on the topic of **types of travel.**

You have done some research and produced a diagram. Using your information and notes, write an interesting and informative article to send to the website. Write between 180-220 words.

Research: Total travellers worldwide

Type of Travel	2007	2013	2019
Cruises	15.6 million	21.1 million	30.4 million
Caravan Tours	10 million	9.8 million	15.7 million
Package Tours	17 million	19 million	23.5 million

Source: mtc.mag

 It can be quite tough to be imaginative and interpret the data, so we'll be kind and give you a few ideas for this first practice.

Think about the type of traveller that might go on each type of trip, and the advantages (comfort, cost, security) and disadvantages (impact on culture, environment) of each type of holiday.

 After you have written your responses, check them against the model answers (C2 level) on our e-learning platform then write an improved version yourself.

aptis academy.com

The UK Economy

Quite Interesting (QI.com) is a website that welcomes articles from readers on topics of general interest. You have decided to submit an article on the topic of **the UK economy.**

You have done some research and produced a diagram. Using your information and notes, write an interesting and informative article to send to the website. Write between 180-220 words.

Research: The UK economy

	2010	2019
Gross Domestic Product ($)	$1.6 trillion	$2.4 trillion
Unemployment Rate (%)	4.5%	15.1%
National Debt (% of GDP)	36.8%	84%

Source: statista.com

We've included this task on economics (always unpopular) as there are articles in the real test on this topic and many students find it particularly difficult as they worry they know nothing about economics. Don't worry, neither do we! What's important is our **interpretation of the data,** so spend some time looking at the data and ask yourself the following questions:

1. Which of the criteria are positive for a country, and which are negative?
2. Can you identify any trends?
3. What impact might the changes have on the citizens of the UK? What might be the consequences of the changes to daily life?

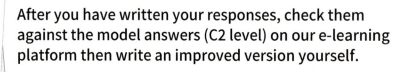

After you have written your responses, check them against the model answers (C2 level) on our e-learning platform then write an improved version yourself.

aptis academy**.com**

In this part you will chat to a member in a social network chat.
You should write 30-40 words.
You should spend a <u>maximum of 10 minutes</u> on this task in the exam.

TASK 1

 You are a new member of a fashion club. You are chatting to another member in the online club chat room. Write 30-40 words per response.

> Hey there! I see that you have recently become a member of our fashion club. Would you mind sharing why you decided to join?

> Where do you get your style inspiration from?

> Have you heard that the club is going to organise trips to London to attend fashion shows? What do you think of the idea?

TASK 2

>> In this part you will read an email and write a response.
You need to respond to the email in 120-150 words by using the notes provided and expressing how you feel about the situation.
You should spend a <u>maximum of 15 minutes</u> on this task in the exam.

RESTAURANT FEEDBACK

Dear Customer,

In an attempt to improve our restaurant and offer a better service to our customers, we are requesting feedback from our most valued clients.

We would appreciate your feedback on our restaurant interior, our facilities and the variety of products we offer.

Many thanks for your collaboration.

Kind regards,
The Management

My notes:
1. Lights too bright
2. Toilets dirty/no toilet paper!
3. Poor choice/menu

TASK 3

In this part, you will write an article for a website which is informative and interesting. You will be given notes and data on which to base your article. The article needs to be between 180 - 220 words.
You should spend <u>about 20 minutes</u> on this task in the test.

Electric Vehicles

Quite Interesting (QI.com) is a website that welcomes articles from readers on topics of general interest. You have decided to submit an article on the topic of **electric vehicles.**

You have done some research and produced a diagram. Using your information and notes, write an interesting and informative article to send to the website. Write between 180-220 words.

My notes:
- **Advantages:** no fuel needed, government grants available, no road tax
- **Disadvantages:** more expensive, kilometre limit, not enough recharging points

Vehicle Research

	2018	2019	% change
Diesel	653,786	515,054	-21.2%
Petrol	1,278,625	1,306,97	-2.2%
Full electric	12,555	28,256	+125.1%
Hybrid	25,982	26,557	+1.7%

SPEAKING COMPONENT

» The speaking component consists of four tasks and lasts for <u>12 minutes.</u> The level of difficulty of the tasks increases as the test progresses. You will have a paper and pen to make notes.

 TASK 1: COMPARE TWO PICTURES

In this part, you will be shown **two photographs** and asked to **compare and contrast** them. You will then be asked **two more questions on the same theme** as the photographs.

You will need to speak for **45 seconds for each** of the three questions.

 TASK 2: TWO-MINUTE LONG TURN

In this part, you will be asked to speak for **2 minutes** about a **personal experience or memory**. There are **three** questions to answer which are all related to the same experience or memory.

You will have a **minute to prepare**, before speaking for **2 minutes**.

 TASK 3: TOPIC PRESENTATION

In this part, you will be shown a **statement** and **several arguments in favour and against.** You must present both sides of the argument by choosing two points in favour and two against.

You will have a **minute to prepare**, before speaking for **1 minute 30 seconds.**

 **TASK 4: TOPIC QUESTION**

In this part, you will be asked a **more complex question** which is connected to the theme of the topic presentation in task 3.

You will have to respond quickly as you are **not given any preparation time** for this final task. You have to speak for **45 seconds** to answer the question.

S1: COMPARE TWO PICTURES

In this part, you will be shown two pictures and answer three questions. You have 45 seconds to respond to each question.

 Study the model answers on the platform for ideas, advanced vocabulary, structures and correct timing.

DESCRIBE

The **first question** will ask you to describe the pictures, so **compare** and **contrast** them

Use the structures included in the tutorial to help you.

SPECULATE

The **second question** often asks you to **speculate** about **themes** represented in the photos.

This could include talking about the **advantages and disadvantages** or discussing **what it would be like** to be there.

MAKE A CHOICE

The **third question** will usually ask you to **make a choice**.

You may have to **decide** between the photographs or **choose** what you would prefer.

QUESTION 1: Tips and Strategies

DESCRIBE

Give a general description of what you can see in the first picture.

In the first picture we can see..

What are the people doing?
Where was the photo taken?
What else can you see?

SPECULATE

Now you can speculate about the first photograph.

I would say that..
Perhaps..
Maybe..
It might be..

Then explain why.

Now you can move to the **second photo** by using
a connecting word or phrase.

..whereas..
..while..
..whilst..
..in contrast..

DESCRIBE

SPECULATE

Give a general description of what
you can see in the second picture.

Now you can speculate about the
second photograph.

In the second picture we can see..

What are the people doing?
Where was the photo taken?
What is in the background or
foreground?

I would say that..
Perhaps..
Maybe..
It might be..

Then explain why.

 Practise completing this part in 45 seconds.
In the exam you will be able to see the time on the screen.

 Don't spend too much time on the first photo before using a connecting word or
phrase and passing to the second photo.

QUESTION 2: Tips and Strategies

If you are asked about the advantages and disadvantages of something you can **paraphrase** this by using the words and expressions used by **native speakers.**

upsides and downsides
benefits and drawbacks
pros and cons

If you are asked about **why something is important** or **why people like** something you should structure your answer and **explain your reasons** clearly.

The main reason that..is important is..

Another reason people like..might be because..

 By using different words from the question you can show the examiner that you can use a range of vocabulary.

QUESTION 3: Tips and Strategies

If the final question asks you to **make a choice** you could use a conditional sentence to start your answer.

"I like both situations, but if I had to decide, I'd probably choose..because.."

After that, you can talk about your **life** and **past experiences**. You don't need to mention the photos anymore.

 By structuring your answer clearly you will make your response easy to understand and you will get a higher level.

Practice 1

1 Tell me what you can see in the two pictures.
2 Is it important to preserve different customs?
3 Which celebration would you prefer to attend?

45 SECONDS
EACH
QUESTION

Practice 2

1 Tell me what you can see in the two photographs.
2 What skills might be needed in these professions?
3 Which of these jobs would you prefer to do?

45 SECONDS
EACH
QUESTION

Practice 3

1 Tell me what you can see in the two photographs.
2 What might it be like to travel to both places?
3 Which landscape do you prefer?

45 SECONDS
EACH
QUESTION

Practice 4

1 Tell me what you can see in the two photographs.
2 What are the advantages of eating out and eating in?
3 Do you prefer cooking at home or eating out?

45 SECONDS
EACH
QUESTION

1. Tell me what you can see in the two photographs.
2. What would it be like for the kids in these photos?
3. Which situation would be the most memorable?

45 SECONDS
EACH
QUESTION

Remember that all the speaking tasks in this book have
example model answers on our e-learning platform.

aptis academy.com

S2: TWO-MINUTE LONG TURN

In this part, you need to answer three questions, but in a mini-presentation. You need to speak for 2 minutes, and you have <u>1 minute</u> <u>preparation</u> time.

Study the model answers on the platform for ideas, advanced vocabulary, structures and correct timing.

ANSWER ALL THREE QUESTIONS

You will be asked to speak about **three** points/questions.

You must give an answer to **all three points** and **develop** your response to get a high score for this task.

STRUCTURE YOUR RESPONSE

As you have to speak for **2 minutes** continuously, you need to **structure** your response to give a mini-presentation.

This means you need a **beginning**, **middle** and **end**.

TIMING

Timing is important in this section.

If you don't fully answer all the points/questions, you will be awarded a **lower level**.

💬 MINI-PRESENTATION: Tips and Strategies

You will be given 1 minute to prepare your answer, so quickly write down any vocabulary or expressions you would like to use in your response. Try and think of the less common vocabulary items you know to use in your description.

To score a C1/C2 level you need to keep speaking for the full 2 minutes, so we recommend following these timings (approximately):

Question 1 (speak for 1 minute)
Question 2 (speak for 30 seconds)
Question 3 (speak for 30 seconds)

 2 MINUTES TOTAL

You should practise with a timer/stopwatch before the exam.

**2 MINUTES
TOTAL**

1 Tell me about a time you received some good news.
2 Why was it so important to you?
3 Do you think there is too much bad news in the media?

🗩 MINI-PRESENTATION: Structure

QUESTION 1	QUESTION 2	QUESTION 3
Okay, so a time I received some good news was...	Moving to the second question...	Finally, I think that...
Regarding the first question...	With reference to the second question...	Last but not least, I guess that...
Beginning with the first question...	Passing to the next point...	To finish, I imagine that...
	This leads me to the next point...	

Practice 2

2 MINUTES TOTAL

1 Tell me about something you have made yourself.
2 How did you feel after you had completed it?
3 Why is creativity important?

Practice 3

2 MINUTES TOTAL

1 Tell me about a close friend of yours.
2 Why is this person important to you?
3 Are friends as important as family in the modern world?

**2 MINUTES
TOTAL**

1 Tell me about something you have lost.
2 Was it important to you?
3 Do you own anything you consider to be irreplaceable?

Practice 5

**2 MINUTES
TOTAL**

1 Tell me about a famous piece of artwork you have seen.
2 How do you feel about the price of famous artwork?
3 Is artistic talent inherited or can it be learnt?

S3: TOPIC PRESENTATION

In this part you need to speak for <u>1 minute 30 seconds</u> to present both sides of an argument, by choosing two points from each side.

Study the model answers on the platform for ideas, advanced vocabulary, structures and correct timing.

MAKE NOTES

You will be given 1 minute to read the task and **add your own notes**

Add a few of your own ideas in note form.

CHOOSE

Choose **two points** from **each side** of the argument.

Choose whichever you had the clearest ideas about.

STRUCTURE/TIMING

Structuring your answer is absolutely vital for this task.

You only have 90 seconds so you have to practise **getting to the point quickly**.

Practice 1

" All children should be given a smartphone from a young age."

FOR 👍 Can be tracked wherever they are

👍 All the same / none excluded

👍 Can make emergency calls

AGAINST 👎 Damage to eyesight

👎 Dependency

👎 Negative impact on social skills

STRATEGY: PREPARATION TIME

 You have <u>1 minute</u> to prepare, so start by reading the arguments carefully and adding a few words.

FOR 👍 **Can be tracked wherever they are** Parents can locate kid/GPS

👍 **All the same / none excluded** Less chance of bullying in school

👍 **Can make emergency calls** Emergency services/accident

AGAINST 👎 **Damage to eyesight** More kids wearing glasses nowadays

👎 **Dependency** Kids addicted to phones/apps/games/social media

👎 **Negative impact on social skills** Chat more on social media than in real life

©aptisacademy.com

 Now choose two points from the FOR list, and two from the AGAINST list.

FOR 👍 **Can be tracked wherever they are** Parents can locate kid/GPS

👍 **All the same / none excluded** Less chance of bullying in school/all equal

AGAINST 👎 **Damage to eyesight** More kids wearing glasses nowadays

👎 **Dependency** Kids addicted to phones/apps/games/social media

©aptisacademy.com

 You will be given a piece of paper in the test which you can make notes on. You're going to need to make a lot of notes for the writing tind speaking sections so use the paper wisely.

 IMPORTANT

1. You must only present **2 arguments from each side**, do not talk about all the points mentioned.
2. You have **not been asked your personal opinion**, so there's no need to give your point of view.
3. The points you are given are deliberately **not full sentences**, so you must add any auxiliary verbs, subjects,prepositions and pronouns.
4. You must be **clear and concise.** Do not ramble on and repeat yourself if you want to score highly.
5. You must mention **all four arguments** to complete this task.

STRATEGY: SIX STEPS

STEP 1: INTRODUCE THE TOPIC

" So, regarding the question of whether...all kids should be given a smartphone...there are several arguments in favour and others against."

" The argument of whether... all children should be given a mobile... is a disputed one, and there are points in favour and points against."

" Whether or not...children should be given a phone... is a hot potato. I'm going to outline the key arguments in favour and against."

 Start immediately with an opening phrase to introduce the topic. Any of these can be adapted for any task. ☺

 These are the six steps we recommend you follow to complete this task well. You're going to need to **practise** this task **many times** using our expressions (or your own) to be able to perform well under pressure during the test.

"**Firstly, taking the point that** parents can locate their kids, this is a clear upside for worried parents as they can use a GPS to find their offspring at any time."

Notice how we are presenting the argument we have been given, then developing it a little with our own ideas.

We have about 15 seconds per argument, so we need to be clear and concise and not repeat ourselves.

©aptisacademy.com

STEP 3: PRESENT YOUR FIRST ARGUMENT "AGAINST"

"**Although, it could also be argued that** the constant use of small screens is having a detrimental effect on children's eyesight. In fact, studies show that more kids are wearing glasses than ever before."

We have used a conjuction to express contrast, then mentioned our "AGAINST" point and supported it with some evidence.

©aptisacademy.com

You need to practise being concise and clear to score highly in this task. Our advice is to mention the point and then expand on it with an idea of your own.

"**Moving on to the idea that** if all children have smartphones no kid will be excluded, this argument has some merit. In the past, kids in school were bullied for being the only one without a TV - this is the same problem, just updated. "

We now move on to present another argument in favour.

©aptisacademy.com

STEP 5: PRESENT YOUR FINAL ARGUMENT "AGAINST"

"**Nevertheless, critics might argue that** all this mobile phone and technology use is having a terrible impact on kids. Every day I see young children given phones or tablets by their parents to entertain them. This could surely become addictive in the future."

Notice that we introduce our own experiences, but we don't bother saying "I think this" or "I think that" - there's no time!

©aptisacademy.com

It's better to follow the sequence FOR-AGAINST-FOR-AGAINST as it allows you to use high-level contrasting expressions.

"So, in a nutshell, we could say that it's a good idea for parents and to avoid bullying, but it could lead to poor eyesight and addiction when they grow up."

The most important thing is to complete the task by mentioning the 4 arguments, but if you have a few seconds left it's very impressive to summarise both sides in a few words.

©aptisacademy.com

TIMING

Timing is quite difficult in this task, but you can see from this example that you only need to mention the point and add some of your own words.

We recommend approximately **15** seconds for each of the **steps 1-6.**

©aptisacademy.com

During the test, you will be able to see a timer (like the one in the picture above) in the top right-hand corner of the computer screen. You'll need to **keep one eye on this at all times** during the speaking component of the test.

USEFUL EXPRESSIONS TO MOVE BETWEEN IDEAS

"Firstly, taking that point that..."

"Moving on to the idea that..."

"This brings me to the next point which is..."

"This is connected to the next argument..."

"However, it could be argued that..."

"That said, the downsides are that..."

"Nevertheless, critics might argue that..."

"Although, some might point to the fact that..."

©aptisacademy.com

USEFUL EXPRESSIONS TO SUMMARISE

"So, in a nutshell, we could say that..."

"All things considered, it seems that..."

"All in all, it's clear that..."

"To summarize, I'd say that..."

Remember that it doesn't matter if you don't have time to summarise your arguments - it's just impressive if you do! ☺

All these expressions should be followed by just a few words as in the example. Don't start repeating all the arguments again.

©aptisacademy.com

We've included lots of examples of phrases you can use and adapt to develop your own structures, but this isn't a definitive list so feel free to use your own.

"Everyone should be vegetarian."

FOR 👍 Fewer animals means less CO_2

👍 Farmland can be reforested

👍 No more animal suffering

AGAINST 👎 Lack nutrients

👎 Humans natural carnivores

👎 Can't grow veg easily in dry countries

Practice 3

90 SECONDS

"CCTV cameras reduce crime and make our city safer."

FOR 👍 Evidence used in court

👍 Cheap and easy to install

👍 Act as a deterrent

AGAINST 👎 High crime rates in cities with many cameras

👎 Evidence not valid (cover faces)

👎 Invasion of privacy

Practice 4

90 SECONDS

" The government is responsible for environmental protection."

FOR 👍 Can negotiate international cooperation

👍 Controls public spending and taxation

👍 Regulates big business

AGAINST 👎 Collective action leads to real progress

👎 Governments change every 4 years

👎 Small changes make biggest impact

Practice 5

90 SECONDS

" Technological change means progress."

FOR 👍 Makes life easier

👍 Medical advances thanks to tech

👍 Improved global communications

AGAINST 👎 Used for weapons and war

👎 Some find it difficult to use

👎 Society becoming dependent

In this part you need to answer a complex, often profound question and give your opinion.

You have to speak for 45 seconds and you have <u>no preparation time</u>.

RESPOND

As this is always a difficult or profound question to answer, you can first **acknowledge** the **complexity** of the problem.

OPINION

Then you should give your opinion on the topic in a **clear and concise** way.

There are only 45 seconds, so you're not really expected to solve the problem.

EVIDENCE

It's a good strategy to support your opinon briefly with a **case study**, **example**, or something from your **personal experience**.

Practice 1

Do you think the concept of 'childhood' has changed over the years?

The question for task 4 will be connected to the theme in task 3.

STRATEGY: DEVELOPING A COHERENT RESPONSE

USEFUL EXPRESSIONS TO START YOUR RESPONSE

"I think that it's a complex issue, but…"

"I would say that it depends on the (situation, person), but…"

"This is the type of question that requires a deep analysis of all the factors. That said, I'd say…"

"It's curious, as I was reading an article about this just the other day…"

"I'll admit I've never given it much thought before, but…"

USEFUL EXPRESSIONS TO GIVE OPINIONS

"Based on the evidence we have at the moment, it would seem…"

"I imagine that most people would say…, whereas I believe that…"

"To my mind, it seems that…"

"Looking at it from a (Western, biased) perspective, I'd say that…"

"All things considered, I guess that…"

 We have included here some useful expressions to give you ideas, but this is not a definitive list, so feel free to use your own ideas.

"Taking the case of (Spain) as an example, we can see that…"

"I can only speak from personal experience, but…"

"There are many studies which have shown that…"

"A good example to support this might be…"

©aptisacademy.com

Practice 2

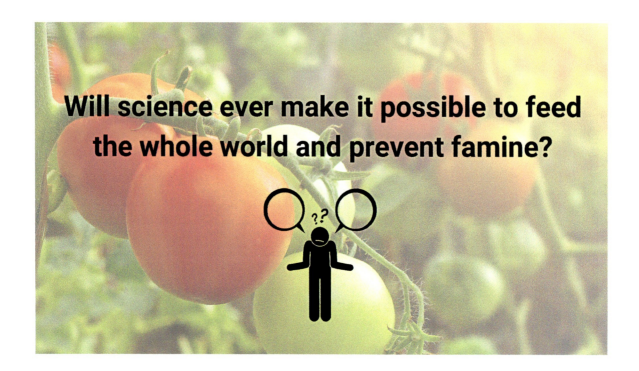

Will science ever make it possible to feed the whole world and prevent famine?

Think about scientific discoveries that have made food more plentiful in the West. Will famine ever be eradicated in the developing world?

 Focus here on if police are 'more effective' , so your answer should clearly state which you think works best to reduce crime. It's also a good idea to include some high level 'crime' vocabulary such as pickpockets, mugging, crime rates and public safety.

Practice 4

 Conservation and the environment are popular topics in the test, so you should study related vocabulary and read a few articles on the theme to be well-prepared.

Do you think we should put limitations on future technological development?

 This is basically an ethical question asking if we should have any laws or regulations in place, or if we should allow progress to go unchecked.

 Remember that all the speaking tasks in this book have example model answers on our e-learning platform.

FULL SPEAKING TEST

In this part you will be shown two pictures and answer three questions. You have 45 seconds to respond to <u>each question</u>.

1 Tell me what you can see in both pictures.

2 What would the working environment be like for these jobs?

3 What would your ideal working environment be?

TASK 2 2 mins

In this part you need to answer three questions, but in a mini-presentation. You need to speak for 2 minutes, and you have <u>1 minute preparation</u> time.

1 Tell me about a time you asked for help.

2 Was the help useful?

3 Why is it important to ask for help?

TASK 3 🕐 1 minute 30 seconds

» In this part you need to speak for 90 seconds to present both sides of an argument by choosing two points from each side. You have <u>1 minute preparation time</u>.

" Travelling is the best way to spend your time and money."

FOR 👍 Discover new cultures

👍 Great memories

👍 See life from a new perspective

AGAINST 👎 Negative effect on local area

👎 Tiring

👎 Bad for the environment

TASK 4 🕐 45 seconds

» In this part you have 45 seconds to answer a complex, often profound question and give your opinion. You have <u>no preparation time.</u>

Is truely sustainable tourism really possible?

CORE COMPONENT KEY: TEST 1

GRAMMAR PRACTICE 1

1. A – hope (hope to + infinitive expresses the **future desire of the speaker**)
2. C – soon (as + **adjective** + as, the moment that)
3. C – to inform (formal expression used to give **bad news**)
4. B – whether (whether or **not**)
5. A – was (insisted the last interviewee + **past simple**)
6. C – allowed (to be allowed to do something is to have **permission**)
7. A – has (CHILD is **third person singular**)
8. A – have (**a number of** + students is **plural**)
9. C – an (**before vowel sounds** in English)
10. C – a (to have **a fear of + noun**)

11. A – somebody (**positive** statement)
12. B – Not (part of fixed expression. **Not a single + person/thing**)
13. B – little (**little + uncountable noun** means a small quantity of something)
14. A – Whoever (addressed to **all people who want to participate**)
15. B – invested (It's about time + **past simple**)
16. A – was going (used with BUT to give an **excuse**)
17. C – have been dating (**present perfect** as it started in the past and continues to be true in the present)
18. C – may (**modal verb** used to be **polite**/formal)
19. C – needn't (it is **not necessary**)
20. A – isn't (**question tag**)
21. B – so am I (response used to agree with a **positive statement**)
22. A – long (used to ask **how much time it takes** to do something)
23. C – saw them (saw + **direct object**)
24. A – at (sit **at** the table)
25. C – more boring (**comparative** form)

VOCABULARY PRACTICE 1

1. H - grin	6. C - admire	11. F - filthy	16. G - bill	21. A - light
2. D - giggle	7. H - enhance	12. H - reliable	17. E - conclusions	22. B - metal
3. E - shock	8. A - inhale	13. J - quick	18. B - have	23. I - value
4. G - hurt	9. G - go	14. C - wealthy	19. F - bursts	24. D - obvious
5. J - swap	10. J - evaluate	15. A - economical	20. H - heart	25. G - news

CORE COMPONENT KEY: TEST 2

GRAMMAR PRACTICE 2

1. B – love having (love/like + **ing**)

2. C – any (**hardly any** means **almost none**)

3. A – due to (**to be due to** is used to express a future action that is **expected to happen**)

4. A – leaves (present simple for **transport schedules**)

5. C – provided (**conjunction** with a similar meaning to **if/on the condition**)

6. C – had protested (It was the first time + **past perfect**)

7. A – should you (under no circumstances + **auxiliary** + **subject** + **main verb** = INVERSION)

8. B – as soon as (the minute that)

9. C – shouldn't (modal verb used to give **advice**)

10. B – a bit of (a bit of/a small quantity of + **uncountable noun**)

11. C – where (relative pronoun used with **places**)

12. A – is currently appearing (is now acting or is **now performing.**)

13. C – is considering (present continuous, **thinking about** something **carefully**)

14. A – spent (past simple, **series of actions** in the past)

15. C – must (modal verb of deduction that expresses a **high degree of certainty**)

16. A – should (modal verb used in a formal context to **sound more polite**)

17. B – you (subject + promised + **direct object**)

18. C – are (people **are = plural**)

19. B – both of which (**positive** sentence, referring to the **two languages**)

20. A – receiving (look forward to + **gerund**)

21. A – won't (**tag question** to check information)

22. B – absolutely (**adverb** used with **non-gradable/extreme adjectives**)

23. A – so as not (so as not + **infinitive**, in order not to)

24. B – In spite of (In spite of + noun, gerund, pronoun)

25. A – where he is (indirect question word+ **subject** + **verb**)

VOCABULARY PRACTICE 2

1. B - prize	6. G - sleepy	11. D - rehearse	16. E - appetite	21. C - rise
2. F - salary	7. C - thin	12. A - comprehend	17. H - divorce	22. E - wreck
3. I - evaluation	8. A - thorough	13. I - study	18. I - officers	23. H - ache
4. A - fee	9. E - hairy	14. B - spread	19. B - song	24. B - glass
5. J - globe	10. H - beautiful	15. C - prompt	20. A - problem	25. I - bulb

CORE COMPONENT KEY: TEST 3

GRAMMAR PRACTICE 3

1. C – unless (conjunction to mean **except under the circumstances**)

2. A – stay (subjunctive, recommend that + **infinitive**)

3. B – smell (**present simple**)

4. C – Does he want (present simple **question**)

5. A – was snowing (**past continuous**)

6. C – for (present perfect + **for** + 5 years)

7. B – ever (used with **question forms** with **present perfect** to ask about **life experiences**)

8. A – I have been working (present perfect continuous)

9. C – since (present perfect + **since** + year it began)

10. B – shouldn't she (**question tag** to check for agreement)

11. A – had taken (**past perfect simple**)

12. C – used to (used for **past** states)

13. A – on (for **days and dates**)

14. B – will be sunbathing (future perfect continuous)

15. B – were (**second conditional** for **imaginary situations**)

16. B – should have gone (**should** + **have** + **past participle** to criticize)

17. C – breaking (denied + **gerund**)

18. A – had known (**third** conditional)

19. A – will (**first** conditional)

20. A – would arrive (**reported speech**)

21. C – how long we have (indirect question, I wonder + how long + **subject** + **verb**)

22. B – eating (fancy + **gerund**)

23. A – to stay (decide + **to** + **infinitive**)

24. A – I'm afraid not (**indirect** and **polite** way of saying '**no**')

25. C – I am used to (**I am** used to + **gerund** = accustomed to)

VOCABULARY PRACTICE 3

1. J - staff	6. C - whisper	11. B - workaholic	16. A - luggage	21. A - hours
2. E - ship	7. E - worship	12. A - a hit single	17. B - sting	22. F - pillow
3. A - fire	8. H - argue	13. F - overrated	18. F - living	23. H - surface
4. G - customer	9. A - flood	14. G - ruined	19. I - shift	24. G - meal
5. H - novel	10. I - return	15. D - breathtaking	20. G - leave	25. C - rain

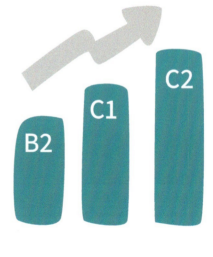